SOCIAL SECURITY DISABILITY LAW

A Reference for Social Security Disability Claims

by

David Daggett and Griff Shuler

DAGGETT SHULER
ATTORNEYS AT LAW

SPEAKER MEDIA PRESS

Social Security Disability Law: A Reference for Social Security Disability Claims

ISBN 978-1-935411-22-2

Contents

CONTRIBUTING AUTHORS

This book is a collective effort compiled for you by twenty leading members of the plaintiff's bar in states across the US. Each attorney involved has contributed his or her expertise to this project to assure the reader that they are being provided with basic sound information as they find themselves seeking Social Security Disability benefits. This is not a law book, but an overview of social security disability law.

A Special thanks to our Copy Editors:
Kevin Pistiner
Alyson Wright

DISCLAIMER

This publication is designed to provide general information regarding Social Security Disability law and is not intended to be legal advice. It is sold and distributed with the understanding that neither the publisher, nor the authors, nor the contributors, are engaged in rendering legal or other professional services to the reader. If legal advice or other professional assistance is required, the services of a competent professional person should be sought.

The publisher, authors and contributors make no representations or warranties with respect to the accuracy or completeness of the contents of this work and specifically disclaim all warranties, including without limitation warranties of fitness for a particular purpose. No warranty may be created by sales or promotional materials. The advice and strategies contained herein may not be suitable for every situation. Neither the publisher, nor the authors, nor the contributors shall be liable for damages arising herefrom.

As this publication is not intended as legal advice, any use of this information will not create an attorney-client relationship. After an initial consultation, and before representing you on any claim, a written attorney-client agreement must be signed in order to create such a relationship.

INTRODUCTION

At Daggett Shuler, Attorneys at Law, we are dedicated to helping disabled individuals who need assistance applying for Social Security Disability benefits. This is not just an empty promise, it is our reason for existing. We are passionate about obtaining the most benefits that you can receive from the Social Security Administration. Our firm only handles cases on behalf of seriously impaired people seeking Social Security Disability benefits. We are proud to say that we have helped thousands of clients receive the Social Security Disability benefits they so desperately needed. They were able to pay necessary expenses, medical bills, and were able to support their families, while they were suffering from debilitating medical problems.

At Daggett Shuler, Attorneys at Law, our firm is rooted in a desire to help people, and we work diligently to do this in a way that exhibits the utmost care and respect for our clients. We have a team of eight lawyers assisted by an experienced professional staff.

Our lawyers are all very distinguished in their own right, but what sets Daggett Shuler apart from many other law firms is the fact that we have been working together for a long time. With more than a hundred years of combined experience practicing law and eighty years of combined experience as a firm, our team has a compatibility rarely seen in the industry. Our continuity puts us in a unique position to help people in a wide variety of situations. Each member of our team possesses unique strengths and specializations, so our clients can be sure that their claim is being considered from a range of angles and aspects.

About Our Firm

"I liked the personal care and one-on-one time at Daggett Shuler. They always had time for me. Daggett Shuler is like part of my family and handled my case with professional care."

-Deborah I.
Burlington, NC

Our firm has a strong dedication to respect and a commitment to developing a personal relationship with our clients. And, since relationship-building is a two-way street, we thought it would be helpful to start out by giving you a brief glimpse into our team: who they are, what their areas of strength are, and how they are completely dedicated to helping people who have been hurt and who are struggling through a complicated justice system.

David D. Daggett

David is the Managing Partner of Daggett Shuler. He has practiced personal injury law since 1985. He is experienced in assisting clients with all types of injury cases, including serious injury, wrongful death, and insurance claims.

Every day at 5 a.m., David is up and running—literally. He's a serious triathlete who has completed more than 160 triathlons, including 24 Ironman competitions. He has completed the Hawaii Ironman World Championship seven times. To his clients, David brings the same intensity and devotion that has helped him become a world-class athlete. "To me, a lot of what I do athletically is a metaphor for what I do professionally," he says. "Both take dedication and planning and there are clear goals and finish lines."

Griffis C. Shuler

Griff is a Partner and Manager at Daggett Shuler, and he is a Board Certified Specialist in Workers' Compensation Law. He concentrates his practice in Workers' Compensation claims and complex third party cases. Griff enjoys educating injured workers regarding their legal rights. He regularly gives seminars on issues involving Workers' Compensation cases. Griff has extensive experience in handling many different types of workers' compensation claims before the North Carolina Industrial Commission.

John K. Koontz

John is a Partner with Daggett Shuler. His practice is devoted to helping disabled individuals obtain the benefits to which they are entitled. John works with Social Security claimants to help them obtain Social Security Disability Benefits and Supplemental Security Income. John also works with individuals who have filed claims for short and/or long-term disability benefits under private disability policies or through their employer sponsored benefit plans. John regularly gives seminars on Social Security Disability benefits and employer sponsored or ERISA Long-Term Disability claims.

Douglas E. Nauman

Doug is a Partner and is the chief negotiator for personal injury cases at Daggett Shuler. He concentrates his practice in serious personal injury liability claims, with particular emphasis in insurance law and alternative dispute resolution. He has specific interest and experience in insurance coverage and insurance policy issues.

Doug has worked in the areas of finance and insurance since 1984, most extensively in the area of automobile insurance coverage and claims. Doug previously worked for State Farm Insurance as a Claim Specialist.

Julie L. Bell

Julie is a Partner with the firm and will likely be the first attorney you speak with if you have a personal injury case. Julie coordinates all new client contact and orientation. Julie also is our foremost authority on medical liens, reimbursement rights, Medicare and Medicaid. She is well-known in the legal community for her seminars and authorship on disbursement issues involving personal injury settlements and awards. Her work is critical to our clients' maximizing their personal injury recoveries.

Thailer A. Buari

Thailer is the newest attorney at Daggett Shuler. A recent graduate of Wake Forest University School of Law, Thailer has worked as a law clerk at the firm since 2013. Thailer works on all aspects of claims in the Personal Injury department from case sign-up to settlement.

Christopher M. Wilkie

Chris handles all aspects of Workers' Compensation claims, and he represents injured workers in both accepted and denied claims. Chris is a Partner with the firm and has worked with David Daggett and Griff Shuler since 2003.

Chris works hard to make sure that his clients understand the processes and procedures involved in Worker's Compensation claims. He has successfully concluded many cases for employees injured in all types of accidents on the job.

Michael W. Clark

Mike is a Partner with the firm and is a litigation and personal injury attorney with Daggett Shuler. He has extensive trial experience in many areas of litigation including personal injury, all types of accidents, construction law, head and brain injuries, truck accidents, motorcycle accidents, construction accidents, wrongful death, injuries from defective products, premises liability, complex medical claims, and civil litigation.

Not only does Mike have considerable litigation experience, but he adds to that his extensive medical background. Mike is a registered nurse and is well-versed in the knowledge necessary to properly understand and advocate our clients' personal injury cases. He has a passion for protecting the rights of those individuals injured by the negligent conduct of others.

As you can see, our lawyers are each well-versed in different types of law and they each have other professional experience, training, and background that they bring to each client's case. This creates the perfect environment in which we are able to all come together with our diverse areas of expertise in order to obtain the best result that we possibly can for our clients. Team members frequently cross practice areas in order to contribute their skills and strengths to better serve our clients.

Customer Service

"Every moment that I spent at Daggett Shuler was special. They have gone above and beyond to comfort me while I was going through the worst time in my life. The support that they have given me cannot be described. I would like to thank Shelia for her incredible effort doing her best, being my friend, and I also felt she was my doctor when I was in a critical situation. Thank you for everything you have done for me. The words cannot describe how happy I am with the service Daggett Shuler has given me and my family."

-Jakup N. from Greensboro, N.C.

There are many personal injury law firms out there—we acknowledge that. What sets us apart—what makes us that needle in the proverbial haystack of Personal Injury firms—is our customer service. Our firm has a set of ingrained values that we all work and live by: Teamwork, Service, and Excellence. We strive to deliver to our clients the care and respect they deserve through these three values. It starts from the very first time a client calls us, or the first time they walk through the front door.

"I appreciated the personal treatment and understanding of my situation and the concern that I was being taken care of all the way around."

-Robert G., Valdese, NC

Obviously, our clients expect us to do well on the case. They can easily research and familiarize themselves with our legal reputation. But what separates us from simply possessing a legal reputation with a running tally of wins and losses is delivering to each and every client the care and respect that we believe they deserve.

"Daggett Shuler law firm has treated me with great respect and looked into all areas of helping me with my case."
-Michael B., N. Wilkesboro, NC

Most of the time, when we first meet clients, they are in a bad situation. Our clients may be disabled, injured in some way, have recently lost a loved one due to someone else's negligence or error. One thing they are not getting at other law firms is *care* and *respect.* Therefore, our firm's mission is to deliver care and respect to people when they find themselves in a place in life that they never could have imagined.

"Everyone was polite, sincere and really cared about me, my problem and helping me. The attorneys and staff at Daggett Shuler were the nicest people I've ever dealt with. They are experienced, professional and really care about people."
-David J., Walnut Cove, NC

Of course, our handling of a client's case involves a substantial amount of legal work. Just as important as the legal work is extending empathy and compassion to our clients in their current, unexpected circumstances. Frequently, by the time they get to us, our clients are all too accustomed to being stuck in automated phone trees and not getting a personal service. Everyday, we try to remind ourselves of the difficult path our clients find themselves on. Once we understand their struggle, it's pretty easy for our attorneys and legal staff to wrap arms of encouragement and support around our clients and take care of them.

"I would recommend Daggett Shuler because they are just like another person easy to talk to. A lot of times when you think of attorneys you

just think of 'stuck up people' that don't understand what's really going on, but Griff Shuler was down to earth and easy to talk to and really understood our concerns."

-Ricqueshia B., Winston-Salem, NC

We survey all of our clients at the end of their cases. And, time after time, we get universally excellent comments and praise. Two very specific, very important words that come up more than any other: care and respect. Delivering the highest level of customer service to our clients is as important to us as any other aspect of our client's case, and often the most important to our clients personally.

"I felt Daggett Shuler handled my case very professionally. I, myself felt treated with kindness and understanding, and that was much appreciated. I could not have asked for better service."

-Julie K., Clemmons, NC

Community Involvement

Our dedication to serving people doesn't stop when we clock out at the end of the day. Every member of our team is dedicated to community enrichment as well.

As a group, we have completed over two decades of sponsoring the Safe Sober Prom Night program. Safe Sober Prom Night was founded in 1991 to encourage teens to stay safe and drug and alcohol free on their Prom Night. Over 450 high schools in North Carolina and South Carolina have participated in the program. Since its inception, more than 500,000 students have signed the Safe Sober pledge. In addition, more than $50,000 has been awarded to schools with the highest rate of participation.

The Safe Sober Prom Night Program creates awareness about the dangers of drugs and alcohol – particularly around Prom time. The program asks students to sign a pledge card promising to stay drug and alcohol free on prom night. High schools across the Carolinas use this program on its own, but many also combine it with other activities including dramatizations of accident scenes involving drunk drivers. Some schools involve their Students Against Drink

Driving (SADD) or drama departments, while others use the prom committee or other enthusiastic students to raise awareness.

Our involvement with Safe Sober Prom Night came about because our firm has a unique perspective in the personal injury legal system. Our firm was in the rare position of seeing the other side of this problem: the results inflicted on families who are forever devastated by a single, terrible incident. Therefore, we decided to address that issue and raise awareness for our community.

In the two decades since we began the program, Safe Sober Prom Night has grown from simply raising awareness of the dangers of drinking and drugs and has evolved into a program encouraging leadership, guidance, and direction for the youth in our community. When the program first started, signing the pledge wasn't the "cool" or "popular" thing to do for most high school students. But over the years, we have worked diligently to develop an environment of awareness and enthusiasm for this cause. Now, there is often a stampede in lunchrooms when we are handing out the program's pledge cards and t-shirts during lunch hour. Students wear the t-shirts as a badge of honor, and since today's youth are tomorrow's community leaders, we firmly believe that enriching our youth now will lead to stronger communities in the future.

In addition, our attorneys also participate in many other community activities outside the firm. Many members of our team are active participants in a broad range of professional leadership roles on the local and state level. The lawyers in our firm serve in leadership roles in local civic groups, church groups, community groups, and more. The focus on service—of serving not just our clients, but our greater community as a whole—has become part of our firm's culture. Our dedication to service is part of what makes us who we are.

How We Can Help

Since we work with disabled people every day, we completely understand how devastating and difficult it can be to live with a debilitating injury or illness. Our clients come to us with all types of serious disabilities, from blood disorders to neurological disorders to brain damage, as well as vision and speech loss. Some of our clients will have to live with these disabilities for the rest of their lives and we are here to ensure they receive the disability benefits they deserve. In addition to the physical pain, the emotional trauma, the shock, and the plain unfairness of this situation, it is often emotionally draining.

On top of all this, our clients and their families typically begin to have serious financial problems as time goes on. With a serious injury, medical bills can easily add up to six figures, a sum that can bankrupt ordinary Americans. (In fact, one recent study found that medical bills are the most frequently cited cause of individual bankruptcy.) Hospitals will usually hold the injured person responsible for paying those bills, which means that victims and their families can be financially crushed if a medical insurance company refuses to do its job. Disabled people may not be able to work to earn an income, and their loved ones are likely to lose income taking care of them.

As Social Security Disability lawyers, our goal and our job is to help solve this problem for disabled people. Pursuing a disability claim will not resolve or cure your medical problem, but it can help pay the astronomical financial costs a disability may cause, including injuries, physical pain, and emotional suffering.

Some people are uncomfortable with the thought of asking for money to compensate them for disabilities. They believe – correctly – that no amount of money will reverse a disability or bring back a loved one to their pre-disabled condition. Instead, the Social Security Disability system uses financial benefits and services as a way to make the disabled individual whole, as much as possible. It may be a flawed system, but we do not believe anyone should be ashamed of using it for its intended purpose, especially if they are suffering financially because of a disability. And we have yet to meet a single client who wouldn't give back all the money, in a heartbeat, if it could erase their disability.

The Social Security Disability process can be challenging and take many months to see any results. This book will give you an overview of the application process and what challenges you may face. The application process involves compiling a well documented case that will be used to prove you are qualified to receive disability benefits. You need to be prepared for any question you may be asked.

This book is useful for people who are in all stages of the application process. It will help people who are just thinking about applying to applicants who have been denied disability benefits. If you are injured or ill you may use this book to find out if you may be eligible for disability benefits. The application process is explained to help you understand the work needed to be completed to apply for disability benefits. It is our hope to help you understand why a Social Security Disability attorney will be your most important asset for winning disability benefits. It can be very disappointing when you lose your disability claim. Daggett Shuler, Attorneys at Law will be able to help you appeal your claim and fight for the benefits you deserve.

Sadly, many Social Security Disability applicants complete the required forms, but they are not granted disability benefits. Applying and appealing your disability claim does not guarantee you will win your case and receive disability benefits. Your attorney will use all the resources available to ensure you receive your disability benefits from the Social Security Disability Administration. He wants you to receive the benefits you deserve to pay for your necessary expenses. When we agree to represent you, we think you have a strong case that may lead to you winning disability benefits.

No highly regarded attorney will guarantee you will receive disability benefits. If you do win your case, the process may take several months or years until you are granted disability benefits by the Social Security Administration. We can promise that we will focus all our energy towards your case to get you the best possible outcome. We have a strong record of successful disability cases and we hope you will give us an opportunity to add your case to our list of success stories.

Many Social Security Disability applicants are living on a very strict financial budget and think they will not have the means to hire an attorney. Legal fees may discourage applicants from the many resources an attorney offers. Our law firm only uses the contingency fee method to pay for our legal representation. You will not have to pay for our services unless you win your case. We never charge you a fee at the beginning of your case. Instead, we are paid using a percentage of the money you receive from the Social Security Administration. If we do not win your case, we will not ask you for any legal fees. This allows us to represent everyone who we feel has a strong case, regardless of their income or financial standing.

Next Steps

This book was written with the hope that it would be a resource for people who suddenly find themselves dealing with the difficult physical, emotional and financial fallout from a serious disability. We hope this book gives you a good overview of Social Security Disability benefits, even if you do not decide to apply.

We know that no book can answer all of your questions about applying for disability benefits. Every case is unique and every client will have questions that can only be answered after we learn more about his or her personal situation. That's why we'd like to invite you to come in and talk to us more about your case. We offer free, confidential initial consultations – meetings at which we discuss your case and its prospects. If you are currently unable to travel, we can bring this meeting to you, whether that means to your home or to a rehabilitation center or even to your hospital bedside.

At a consultation, you can tell us the details of your disability and show us any documentation you might have saved. Then, we can give you our professional opinion about your case and its prospects if you decide to pursue a disability claim. This consultation also gives you an opportunity to interview us and our law firm. Please do not be afraid to ask us questions about our past success stories or other information that might be important to you. We know hiring an attorney is an important decision and we want you to feel completely confident with your decision.

If you want to set up a consultation – or just have questions, comments or concerns – we encourage you to contact us at 1-800-815-5500.

CHAPTER ONE

SOCIAL SECURITY DISABILITY PROGRAMS

Many social security disability applicants are overwhelmed at the thought of the federal disability programs and the complicated application process. To apply for disability benefits applicants need to fill out many forms, compile their medical records, and hope they have a well-documented case, while they are suffering from a debilitating disease or injury. Daggett Shuler, Attorneys at Law will alleviate the stress of worrying about gathering the necessary documentation needed for a complete case. We will guide you through the application process and assure you that you are not alone. Daggett Shuler, Attorneys at Law will be with you will be with you during every step of the process. Before applying for Social Security Disability benefits, you need to understand the different types of disability benefits. This chapter will highlight the federal disability programs and give you an understanding of their differences. Review the different disability programs to determine what program will best suit your disability.

Social Security Disability Insurance (SSDI)

The Social Security Disability Insurance program helps disabled individuals who are unable to continue working at a typical full time job. SSDI is a program run by the federal government and is funded by the Social Security Trust Fund. The program, which was established in 1954, has been helping millions of disabled individuals live a meaningful life without the worries of poverty. Your SSDI benefit will be based on the amount of time you spent working and the salaries that you earned in your past. SSDI members receive a monthly income while they are disabled, to help pay for necessary expenses that otherwise would not be paid. The Social Security Administration requires all disability benefits recipients to prove that their disability will affect their ability to work for a minimum of twelve (12) months or result in death. This does not mean that you need to suffer through your disability for twelve months until you apply for disability benefits. If you believe your disability is predicted to affect you for the next twelve months you may qualify to receive disability benefits.

The SSDI application process is very detailed with intricate questions and instructions to determine if you would be a good candidate to receive SSDI benefits. Many applicants become overwhelmed by the process and as a result do not thoroughly fill out the application. Daggett Shuler, Attorneys at Law will work with you to ensure that all applications are correctly filled out and all necessary information is sent to the Social Security Administration. We can be contacted at 1-800-815-5500. Chapter Five: The Application Process, will discuss the process of applying for disability benefits in detail. The Social Security Administration uses many assessments to determine if you would be qualified for the program. They use three main questions to begin the process: Are you able to work at any of your previous jobs? Are you able to adjust to work at other jobs? Has your disability impacted you or is it expected to impact you for at least twelve months? These questions will be analyzed and defined throughout this book.

Supplemental Security Income (SSI)

Many disabled individuals who have a limited income and a small savings fund may be qualified to receive Supplemental Security Income. The SSI program was created to help disabled or blind adults and children who needed extra resources to maintain a comfortable standard of living. The SSI program is funded by tax dollars collected by the federal government and is separate from the Social Security Trust Fund. SSI applicants are not required to have a work history to receive benefits for their disability. This allows all types of individuals to apply for SSI benefits. You must also be a US citizen to qualify for SSI benefits. The Social Security Administration allows several exceptions to allow people who are not US citizens to qualify for SSI disability benefits. The Social Security Administration requires your disability to affect your ability to work for a minimum of twelve (12) months or result in death. You do not need to suffer through your disability for the twelve months before you apply for SSI benefits. If your disability is expected to last a minimum of twelve months, you can apply for SSI disability benefits. This will reduce the amount of time you must wait until you are granted disability benefits. Discuss your situation with Daggett Shuler, Attorneys at Law and we will help you determine if you may qualify to receive SSI disability benefits.

SSI is designed to be a supplemental income for applicants and encourages members to work while they receive their benefits. Each year the Social Security Administration sets a limit on the amount of income a person may receive, while they are a part of the SSI program. The Federal Benefit Rate (FBR) is established each year based on the cost of living. This rate determines the federal income limit a person may receive while they are awarded SSI benefits. The Social Security Administration also sets a limit on the amount of assets a disability applicant may hold and still qualify to receive disability benefits. This allows disabled individuals the opportunity to continue working and not feel as if they are solely depending on the government to pay their necessary expenses.

Differences between SSDI and SSI

Many applicants of either SSDI or SSI arrive at the same question: What is the difference between Social Security Disability Insurance and Supplemental Security Income? The two programs are similar, but also include several differences. One main difference is that SSDI is funded by the Social Security Trust Fund, while SSI is funded by federal tax revenue. Since the SSDI program is funded by the Social Security Trust Fund, the applicant, their spouse or parent must have worked a specific amount of time. This requirement is needed because the federal government wants an "insured" applicant who has contributed to the Social Security Trust Fund prior to applying. To be eligible for SSI, you must have a limited income and also a limited savings fund. Daggett Shuler, Attorneys at Law will help you determine if you have worked enough time to be eligible for SSDI or if you qualify for SSI based on your income and resources.

SSDI and SSI also provide its members with health insurance coverage, but through different programs. Medicare is provided through SSDI benefits, which is administered by the Social Security Administration. Since SSI is geared towards disabled individuals who have a limited income, they receive health insurance coverage through the Medicaid health plan. Medicaid is a jointly-funded, Federal-State health insurance program that covers disabled or blind children and adults. Monthly benefit payments will vary from person-to-person, but it will also vary between SSDI and SSI. The Social Security Administration determines your benefit amount on the length of time you have worked and your earnings. SSI benefits are determined using a Federal Benefit Rate (FBR), which varies year-to-year. Daggett Shuler, Attorneys at Law will be able to help you calculate the benefit amount you may receive.

Receiving SSDI and SSI Concurrently

Many applicants try to receive benefits from the SSDI program and the SSI program concurrently, but are unsuccessful. Only a few applicants may fit into this category and be entitled to receive both at the same time. You may only receive benefits concurrently if you qualify to receive benefits from both SSDI and SSI. This method of applying can be helpful for applicants who qualify for SSDI, but will not receive a large benefit amount. By also applying to the SSI program you can increase your monthly benefit to the SSI maximum. Determining if you are eligible to receive both SSDI and SSI benefits concurrently can be challenging. Daggett Shuler, Attorneys at Law will help you determine if you qualify to receive SSDI and SSI benefits concurrently. We will also help you get the highest benefit amount you are qualified to receive.

Widow and Widower's Disability Benefits

It can be very tragic to lose a spouse and become a widow or widower. You may have lived many years together and depended on each other for support. It is also heartbreaking when you also become disabled seven years before or after the death of your spouse. This could greatly reduce your income and make it difficult to pay your necessary expenses. Some widows and widowers are able to apply for Social Security Disability benefits. If you meet the requirements to receive disability benefits or are already receiving benefits you may be eligible for a higher monthly benefit. You may receive a higher monthly benefit by including the length of time your spouse worked and paid into the Social Security Trust Fund. This money may be added to your Social Security Disability benefit income and alleviate the stress of worrying if you will have enough disability benefit income to pay all the necessary expenses.

SSI Benefits for Children

It can be a tragic moment when you determine that you must apply for disability benefits for your child. You may be struggling to provide your child with all the resources needed to live a normal life. It is good to know that the Social Security Administration offers disability benefits to children under the age of 18. This program was designed to assist low income families who may not have many resources. Children who are under the age of 18 may qualify to receive Supplemental Security Income (SSI) if his or her income or assets are below a set amount and they are disabled. Since the applicants must be below the age of 18 they would most likely not receive an income or have any assets. The Social Security Administration would determine if the child qualifies for disability benefits based on the parent's income and assets.

When a child under the age of 18 is receiving SSI benefits and he turns 18, he is now considered an adult. At this time the Social Security Administration will not use the child eligibility requirements to determine if the person is able to receive SSI disability benefits. The parent's income and assets would not be relevant in determining if their child is eligible to receive SSI disability benefits. The eligibility requirements would now be based only on the disability benefit recipient's income and assets.

SSI benefit applicants who were not eligible when they were under the age of 18, because of the parent's income and assets, may now qualify when they turn 18. This can give children who have a severe disability an opportunity to receive SSI benefits. It will help to pay for the many expenses that can easily pile up. The parents will also feel relieved that their child will not have to worry about finding a way to pay for their bills. It gives them hope that their child will live a meaningful life.

Adult Child Disability Benefits

A child who became disabled before turning 22, may qualify to receive SSDI benefits even if he or she have never worked. The Social Security Administration uses the parents work history to determine the amount of disability benefits the adult child may receive. Applying for SSDI benefits would increase the child's monthly disability benefits, if he or she is currently receiving SSI benefit, and help to give the child a better life. The main qualification for the child to receive SSDI benefits is if the parent is currently receiving Social Security retirement benefits, is disabled, or is deceased.

CHAPTER TWO

UNDERSTANDING COMMON DISABILITIES

The Social Security Administration has compiled a list of diseases and injuries they may consider for approval of either SSDI or SSI benefits called the Listing of Impairments. The list may be used to become familiar with the many types of diseases and their descriptions. Below is an overview of the different categories that includes some common diseases and injuries. You may find the complete Listing of Impairments on the Social Security Administration's website at www.ssa.gov/disability/professionals/bluebook/.

Blood Disorders

People who suffer from blood disorders may be eligible to receive Social Security Disability benefits. They can affect a person's white blood cells, red blood cells, platelets, and plasma, which all have a specific job to perform within the body. White blood cells help fight off infection, red blood cells distribute vital oxygen throughout the body, platelets help stop bleeding, and our body uses plasma to help balance our electrolytes. It may seem that a blood disorder may not qualify as a disability, but it could affect your daily life. Some common blood disorders that may meet the requirements for Social Security Disability benefits are chronic anemia, chronic thrombocytopenia, hemophilia, leukemia, thrombosis, or sickle cell disease.

Brain Injuries

A traumatic brain injury (TBI) can be a very frightening injury that may not only affect you, but also your family and friends. Brain injuries can occur suddenly and can change a person's life forever. This type of injury occurs when the head has experienced a forceful impact that shakes the brain within the cavity. A brain injury can also occur when the skull is broken open, allowing the brain to be susceptible to damage. Traumatic brain injuries can range from mild to severe and produce many life-changing ramifications. You may qualify for Social Security Disability benefits, which will give you the needed resources to pay important expenses and ensure that you have health insurance for rehabilitation services.

MELANIE'S STORY

Teaching children every day, Melanie inspired her students to want to learn and get them to take pleasure in going to school. One evening Melanie tried to reach a bowl on a high shelf by standing on a kitchen chair. As she grabbed the bowl, the chair broke and Melanie suffered a serious brain injury. This tragic accident caused her to quit her job she loved.
Since Melanie was unable to work, she applied for disability benefits. Unfortunately, she was denied disability benefits, because the Social Security Administration determined that she could still perform unskilled work. They believed she could still hold a job, such as tearing tickets at a movie theater. The SSA did not say, though that there are jobs available. If Melanie decided to hire an attorney to represent her during this stressful time, she might have been able to receive benefits. Her attorney would have argued against the SSA to get Melanie the disability benefits she deserved.

Cardiovascular (Heart) Disorders

The main muscle of the human body, the heart, can produce many life-threatening consequences if not in proper working condition. Cardiovascular disease includes a wide range of heart issues. These can include congenital heart disease that a person is born with, or life-style diseases that were the result of a person's life decisions. Cardiovascular disease can be difficult to determine and Daggett Shuler, Attorneys at Law will be able to determine if you may qualify to receive Social Security Disability benefits. Common cardiovascular diseases that people suffer from are chronic heart failure, coronary artery disease, myocardial infarction (heart attack) and stroke.

Diabetes

Diabetes is a debilitating disease that affects millions of Americans, but it has recently been removed from the list of common Social Security Disabilities. Even though it has been removed, diabetes can have drastic consequences for a person's ability to live a normal life. You must maintain a strict diet and ensure you have access to insulin, which balances your blood glucose levels. You may experience severe side effects if your blood glucose levels change rapidly. This can affect your ability to think or concentrate during a typical job. If you are unable to control your blood glucose levels your body may begin to shut down. This could result in high blood pressure, kidney disease, loss of vision, neuropathy which can cause numbness in the feet, and stroke. These side effects can severely alter your ability to work and could be considered a disability. You may call Daggett Shuler, Attorneys at Law at 1-800-815-5500 to discuss your situation and determine if you may qualify for Social Security Disability benefits.

Immune Disorders

It can be devastating to discover that you have an immune disorder. They can have life changing effects, which could limit your ability to hold a typical job. When an immune disorder enters a person's body, it begins to attack its own tissue. This occurs because your body mistakes itself as a foreign tissue. Side-effects of an immune disorder can result in drastic changes to your life. Some common immune disorders are acquired immune deficiency syndrome (AIDS), human immunodeficiency virus (HIV), immune deficiency disorders, rheumatoid or inflammatory arthritis, Lupus, Raynaud's Disease, Sjogren's Syndrome, and systemic sclerosis.

Mental Health Problems

Disabled individuals who suffer from mental health problems may qualify to receive Social Security Disability benefits if you are unable to hold a job due to this disability. Many people who fall into this category may not have the ability to earn their own money to pay for necessary expenses. Social security disability benefits would give you the security needed to live a more peaceful life knowing that you will not suffer in poverty. Some of the common mental health disabilities that may qualify to receive Social Security Disability benefits are psychotic disorders, such as schizophrenia and paranoia. They may also include affective disorders, anxiety-related disorders such as depression and bipolar disorders, autism, somatoform disorders, and personality disorders. Daggett Shuler, Attorneys at Law will help you through the challenging process fight for your qualified benefits. Call 1-800-815-5500 for a free consultation.

Neurological (Nervous System) Disorders

The nervous system can be classified into two sections: Central Nervous System (CNS) and Peripheral Nervous System (PNS). The Central Nervous System consists of the brain and the spinal cord. The Peripheral Nervous System transmits information from the brain and spinal cord to the rest of the body and back. If you acquire a neurological disorder your ability to work may be affected. Some common nervous system disorders include benign brain tumors, cerebral palsy, epilepsy, Parkinson's syndrome, Multiple Sclerosis (MS), and spinal disorders that have affected your nervous system.

Orthopedic (Muscle, Bone, Joint) Disorders

Orthopedic disorders can affect the musculoskeletal system that relate to the bones, joints, tendons, ligaments, and muscles of the body. Injuries and disorders to these parts of the body can make it difficult for you to move. Your orthopedic disorder can become so severe that it might prevent you from sitting or standing for long periods and affect your ability to work. Some common orthopedic disorders that could lead to loss of function or movement are amputation, back and hip injuries, soft tissue injuries that will require prolonged treatment in excess of twelve months, growth impairments, bone and joint deformity or injury.

Pulmonary (Breathing) Disorders

Pulmonary disorders can be some of the most frightening disorders, because they can affect you at every moment of your day. You may feel out of breath and unable to complete simple tasks due to your pulmonary disorder. You may be able to receive benefits if your disability is found to severely impact your ability to work. Pulmonary disorders are classified into two categories: obstructive breathing disorders and restrictive breathing disorders. Some common obstructive breathing disorders deal with Chronic Obstructive Pulmonary Disease (COPD), such as emphysema, chronic bronchitis, and asthma. Restrictive breathing disorders are those that restrict or reduce a person's lung capacity. These would include diseases of the lungs such as fibrotic lung disease, paralysis of the breathing muscles, and spinal deformities. Sleep-related breathing disorders can cause pulmonary vascular hypertension, which can lead to shortness of breath, dizziness, or fainting.

Skin Disorders

Skin disorders may appear in many forms and may cause permanent damage to your skin or surrounding areas. They may interfere with joint movement or mobility and reduce your ability to work. Some common skin disorders are burns that will require prolonged treatment in excess of twelve months, bullous disease, chronic infections, and dermatitis such as psoriasis, genetic photosensitivity disorders, and ichthyosis.

Vision and Speech Loss

Vision and speech are the two most vital senses of the human body. Vision allows you to discover new sights and see the world around you. Speech gives you the ability to communicate with other people and express your opinion. It can be a life-changing moment when you lose one or both of these vital senses. You may become isolated and do not know where to search for help. The loss of these senses may make you feel trapped and fear that you do not have the ability to fight for yourself. Daggett Shuler, Attorneys at Law is here to help you receive the necessary benefits to live a meaningful life. We are here to break through the isolation and give you the freedom you deserve.

CHAPTER THREE

THE ROLE OF AN ATTORNEY

Your Attorney Fights For You

Daggett Shuler, Attorneys at Law will guide you through the process and take away the stress of the application process. We will compile all the necessary documentation required to give you the best chance of receiving your disability benefits. You have chosen us to represent and fight for your right to Social Security Disability benefits. We do not work for or are affiliated with any government agency. Once you become our client, we will fight together against the Social Security Administration to get you the disability benefits you deserve.

DAVID'S STORY

David, who was 56, has been driving a tractor trailer across the country for many years. He has always enjoyed his job, but lately he has started to experience leg pains. Driving for long periods of time had made David's legs swell up and as a result he was unable to continue working. He tried to apply for other jobs, but all the companies did not want to hire him due to his limited skills and medical problems. David decided the only way he would be able to pay his bills is to apply for disability benefits. When he sent the application to the SSA, David was denied disability benefits.

After receiving the disappointing news, David decided to hire an attorney to fight for the disability benefits he deserved. His attorney began to compile a file of all David's medical records and other supporting evidence needed to win the case. They appealed the case by requesting reconsideration, but this appeal was also denied.

David's attorney then requested a hearing. During the hearing, David's attorney was able to personally explain to the judge that David's disability has severely affected his ability to work. David's attorney asked David to show the judge his legs and how they were painful and swollen. The judge granted David his disability benefits, because the attorney was able to clearly explain how David's disability affected his ability to work.

Walking you Through the Process

Daggett Shuler, Attorneys at Law wants to make the process flow smoothly to allow you to focus on your disability. When you make the first call to our office at 1-800-815-5500, we will begin the free consultation to determine if your case may qualify to receive Social Security Disability benefits. If we feel you have a valid case that may be won, we will begin the application process.

LISA'S STORY

Lisa decided to apply for Social Security Disability benefits, but her medical condition was not on the Listing of Impairments. She thought since her medical condition was not listed the medical expert reviewing her case would deny her disability benefits. Lisa decided to retain an attorney to represent her during the case. Her attorney helped to compare Lisa's medical condition with ones that are on the Listings of Impairments.

The attorney also explained to the SSA how her medical condition affected her ability to work. By having an attorney represent Lisa, the court approved disability benefits saying that her medical condition was equal to medical conditions found on the Listing of Impairments.

The Client is Always the Decision-Maker

Applying for SSDI or SSI can be a very challenging task that involves answering many difficult questions. We are here to help you make the difficult decisions, but you will always be included in the process. You will never lose control of the situation and feel as if you are forced to follow our guidelines. Our goal is to ensure that you win all the Social Security Disability benefits you qualify to receive. We will give you the necessary resources and tools to give you a greater chance of receiving these benefits. You may at times feel overwhelmed and ready to give up by the tremendous amount of paperwork and bureaucracy involved. We will be there to help you, guide you, and encourage you every step of the way towards a successful outcome.

STEPHEN'S STORY

When Stephen was 15, he was involved in a serious car accident. He suffered a brain injury during the accident. Stephen went through months of rehabilitation to regain some of his mental abilities. He was able to return to school, but he was not able to keep up with the rest of the class and was placed into the special education classes.

When Stephen was born, his grandparents decided to set up an investment account and deposit $60,000 for him to use towards his future education. When Stephen turned 18 years old, his parents applied for him to receive SSI disability benefits. They did not take into account Stephen's education fund as an asset when they applied. Stephen was awarded SSI disability benefits on the initial application.

A year after Stephen began to receive disability benefits the SSA learned about Stephen's education fund and suspended his disability benefits. The SSA required Stephen to pay back the benefits he received during the past year. He was also not qualified to receive disability benefits until the $60,000 was used up. If Stephen's parents consulted with an attorney before they applied for disability benefits, they could have set up a special needs trust. The attorney would have advised the family on the correct way to apply for disability benefits without having Stephen's disability benefits revoked. Stephen would then have been able to continue receiving SSI disability benefits.

CHAPTER FOUR

EVALUATING YOUR DISABILITY

Applying for Social Security Disability benefits can be challenging. You need to provide the Social Security Administration with enough evidence showing that you are suffering from a serious injury that does not allow you to work. The documentation and evidence must also show that you will be affected by this disability for at least twelve (12) months or result in death. The Social Security Administration evaluates your disability through several processes and standards, such as the Five-Step Evaluation Process, the Consultative Examination, and Substantial Gainful Activity Standard. This chapter will provide you with an overview of these assessments and ways you may increase your chances of winning your case.

The Five-Step Evaluation Process

When you submit your application for SSDI or SSI benefits you will be evaluated using the Five-Step Evaluation Process. This process is used to determine if you meet the requirements to receive Social Security Disability benefits and what type of benefits you may receive. The Five-Step Evaluation Process is as follows:

Step 1: Are You Involved in Substantial Gainful Activity (SGA)?

The first step to determine if you qualify for disability benefits is to determine your Substantial Gainful Activity (SGA) level. This first step analyzes your current work situation and the amount of money you are making. If you make over a specified income level you may be engaged in Substantial Gainful Activity (SGA), which would make you ineligible to qualify for disability benefits.

Daggett Shuler, Attorneys at Law will help you determine if you meet this requirement. We may be contacted at 1-800-815-5500. If you are found to be making under the maximum level you may continue onto step two of the evaluation process.

Step 2: What Is the Severity of Your Disability and How Long Has it Lasted?

During step two your disability will be analyzed to determine if it has a severe impact on your mental or physical abilities. It must be shown that your disability greatly affects your ability to work. If it is found that your disability is considered "not severe" you may be ineligible to receive disability benefits. You must also show that you have suffered from this disability for at least twelve (12) months, it is expected to last at least twelve (12) months, or your disability will result in death. If you pass the requirements for step two you may continue on through the evaluation process.

Step 3: Does Your Disability Appear on the List of Medical Disabilities?

To qualify for disability benefits your disability must be classified as a severe disability that affects your ability to work. Your disability will be compared to the Social Security Administration's complete list of medically recognizable disabilities that qualify to receive benefits. Chapter Two: Understanding Common Disabilities will give you an overview of some common disabilities that may qualify for Social Security Disability benefits. You may also view the complete listing of impairments on the Social Security Administration's website at www.ssa.gov/disability/professionals/bluebook/.

If your disability is not specifically located on the list of impairments then the reviewer will determine if your disability is "equal" to a listed impairment. To be considered equal the reviewer will determine if your disability is of the same medical severity as a disability on the list of impairments. You may also be considered "an equal" if you have a combination of impairments, which together equal the severity of a listed disability. Even if your disability or a combination of disabilities does not qualify, your case will still continue on to step four of the Five-Step Evaluation Process.

Step 4: Are You Able To Work At Any Of Your Previous Jobs?

During step four, the case reviewer will analyze your employment history for the past fifteen years and determine the abilities needed to work in your past jobs. Your disability will then be compared to the past jobs you once held to determine if you have the ability to successfully work in one of those jobs. The Social Security Administration uses the Residual Functional Capacity Standard (RFC) to make this determination. If you are found capable of successfully working at a substantial past job you will be denied disability benefits. The reviewer does not take into account the amount of job openings that are available. They only determine if you have the abilities needed to work at a certain job. You may contact Daggett Shuler, Attorneys at Law at 1-800-815-5500 to discuss if you may be denied Social Security Disability benefits based on your past employment.

Step 5: Do You Have The Ability To Work At Any Other Job?

The final step of the Five-Step Evaluation Process determines if you are able to work at a substantial job. Based on your current skill level, age, and education, the case reviewer will locate other jobs that you may be qualified to perform. They are not responsible for finding you a specific job opening. The job that they feel you are qualified to work may not be near your location, similar to past salary levels, or up to jobs of your skill level. If it is determined that you have the skills and ability to perform a specific job you will be denied Social Security Disability benefits.

JOSEPH'S STORY

Joseph had worked for a car manufacturer for 15 years and enjoyed his job. He soon started to experience severe back pain that reduced his ability to walk. He immediately visited his primary care physician who ordered a series of tests and discovered a cancerous spinal tumor. Unfortunately, the tumor was unable to be surgically removed, since disturbing it would have risked complete paralysis. Treatments of chemotherapy and radiation successfully helped shrink the tumor and relieved some of Joseph's pain symptoms. Although Joseph received long-term disability benefits through his employer, he also decided to apply for Social Security Disability benefits. Unfortunately Joseph was denied disability benefits. In the letter Joseph received from the Social Security Administration, it stated that although he had been diagnosed with cancer, Joseph's medical condition may improve, and he may well survive.

Joseph decided he would never qualify to receive disability benefits and did not decide to appeal his case. If he consulted with an attorney for advice about his case, his attorney would have helped Joseph appeal his claim and fight for his right to disability benefits. Even though Joseph was denied the first time he applied, it did not mean that he would never be approved for disability benefits. His attorney would have informed Joseph of his rights to appeal his claim.

The Key to Winning: Diaries and Calendars

When you apply for Social Security Disability benefits you need to have substantial evidence proving your disability. Daggett Shuler and you will fight against the many Social Security Administration departments who are the final judges in determining the validity of your claim. A solid case that includes when your disability started and details of your disability will increase your chances of winning. You should keep a diary of your daily struggles, sacrifices and pain produced by your disability. This will show the Social Security Administration approximately when your disability began, which will be used to determine when you will begin to receive disability benefits. It will also show the sacrifices and pain you had to deal with due to your disability. This will help describe the extent to which your disability affected your ability to function. Case reviewers want to know the details of your disability to give them a better understanding of why you deserve to receive benefits.

You may also choose to keep a calendar, separate from other social event calendars, to document your doctor appointments, Social Security Administration phone calls, and other events related to your disability. The calendar may be used as evidence to further prove your disability. Thoroughly documenting your disability will give you a greater chance of winning your case and receiving Social Security Disability benefits.

SARAH'S STORY

Sara was involved in a serious car accident, which resulted in brain damage. The accident made simple tasks very difficult and she was not able to concentrate on what she needed to complete. Sara went through months of therapy to increase her brain function. After the therapy, Sara was not able to regain full brain function. Before she applied for disability benefits, Sara was enrolled in a school geared towards brain injured adults. The school was designed to improve the skills of brain damage victims. Every time Sara enrolled in the school she had to drop out, because she was not able to keep up with the work load.

Sara decided to apply for disability benefits to help pay for her expenses. When she applied, the SSA denied her claim. Applying for Social Security Disability benefits was very challenging for Sara and she decided to hire an attorney to help her appeal her case. Sara's attorney was able to compile a well documented case needed to win. This took the stress of appealing her case away from Sara and allowed her to work on improving her brain function. They also suggested Sara include her school attendance records in her appeals case. This showed the SSA that she was not able to remain in school for a long period of time. With the help of an attorney Sara's appeal was approved and she was able to receive disability benefits.

Disability Determination Services (DDS)

When the Social Security Administration believes you meet the non-medical eligibility requirements to receive disability benefits, your case will be sent to a state agency. The agency in your state is called Disability Determination Services (DDS). They are responsible for compiling all the necessary documentation needed to make an accurate determination of your disability. DDS handles several types of cases: new applications known as initial claims, reconsideration claims, second initial claims, and continuing disability reviews. DDS conducts continuing disability reviews on cases to determine if a disabled applicant's health has improved.

DDS may also diary a case, which puts the file on hold to see how your injury or illness progresses and determine if it will have an ongoing or permanent disability.

When the Social Security Administration sends your case to DDS, it is assigned to a claims examiner. The claims examiner will compile a complete case by obtaining medical records listed on your application, maintain contact with you, and complete other necessary documents. DDS has many types of claim examiners who review cases at different steps in the application process, such as initial claims, reconsideration claims, and continuing disability review. A claims examiner must review and process many claims in a short period of time and may file documents incorrectly. Some of the many decisions claims examiners must make on each case are deciding when your disability started to affect your ability to work, determine your vocational factors including age, education, and work experience, schedule consultative examinations and coordinating your attendance, and contacting your medical sources for your medical records. By contacting Daggett Shuler, Attorneys at Law at 1-800-815-5500 you will have the security of knowing that your case will be handled properly as it travels through the many steps of the claims process.

Consultative Examination (CE)

During your application and review process, DDS may ask you to take part in a Consultative Examination (CE). A CE is an examination of your physical or mental abilities and how they are affected by your disability. This examination may be ordered by your claims examiner when they believe your case does not have enough evidence to prove you have a disability that affects your ability to work. Your case may not have enough evidence for various reasons, such as your medical records do not prove you are disabled, your doctor has not completed the requested records, or your doctor is not a specialist in your type of disability.

During a physical Consultative Examination you will be asked about the history of your disability and how it has impacted your ability to complete everyday tasks. The doctor will also ask if any treatments, including medication have improved your disability. The doctor will conduct a physical examination relevant to your physical disability. A mental Consultative Examination may be completed by a psychologist or psychiatrist. The doctor will determine your ability to follow instructions, your ability to concentrate, and work in a group. You may also be asked if you are taking medications for your mental disability and if it reduces the impact of your disability.

Substantial Gainful Activity (SGA)

When you apply for Social Security Disability benefits you will be asked if you are currently working or if you have just recently stopped working. Each year the Social Security Administration sets the maximum limit an applicant or a person receiving Social Security Disability benefits may earn. Even if you meet the requirements for disability you will still be denied benefits if you earn over the specified income limit. If you have recently stopped working you must show proof that your disability became worse or that help required during your job was no longer available. If you stopped working without a medical reason, you may not qualify to receive Social Security Disability benefits. You must thoroughly review your income to ensure you will qualify to receive the disability benefits you deserve.

CHAPTER FIVE

THE APPLICATION PROCESS

Applying for Social Security Disability benefits can be a very stressful and difficult process. To increase your chances of receiving benefits and to make the process as easy as possible for yourself, you need to keep thorough records. Having all your documents and records organized will help you apply quickly without any major setbacks. This will ensure you are prepared for any information the Social Security Administration may need during the application process. In this chapter we will highlight the four main check points during the application process from beginning to end. This chapter will give you an understanding of what you will be facing in the months to come.

When to File Your Disability Claim?

Many Social Security Disability applicants are not sure of when to start the application process. Some may think they need to wait a certain amount of time after they become disabled. The application process may last many months and you may have to wait even longer until you begin to receive your disability benefits. If you believe your disability will last for at least the next twelve (12) months or result in death and your income has been drastically reduced due to your disability, you should immediately begin the application process. You should not wait around until someone starts the process for you. The earlier you begin the process, the earlier you will receive your disability benefits. Before you apply though, compile all the required documents and forms so you will be prepared to answer any questions asked during the application process.

Filing Your Disability Claim

It is your duty to make the first move and apply for Social Security Disability benefits. Once you initiate the claim, the process to receive disability benefits will begin. Social Security Disability applicants can choose the application process they are most comfortable using. The Social Security Administration gives you three ways to apply for disability benefits:

- You may travel to your local Social Security office and apply in person. This allows you to personally speak to someone at the office and ensure all your information is correctly documented. To find your local Social Security Administration office, you may call their toll-free number at 1-800-772-1213. You should document when you call the Social Security Administration in case they may need verification of when you contacted the agency. This will help you be prepared for any questions you may be asked related to your application.
- You may call the Social Security Administration by phone using their toll-free number at 1-800-772-1213. This allows applicants who are unable to travel to their local Social Security Administration office an opportunity to apply. During the call you may request the documents needed to apply for benefits be sent to you. This gives you time to review the documents at your home without the distractions that may occur at the Social Security Administration's office. You should have copies of all documents you send to the Social Security Administration and when they were sent to have an organized application process.
- The third way to apply for disability benefits is on the Social Security Administration's website at www.ssa.gov. This gives you access to begin the application process from your home and thoroughly fill out all required information. This may make the process faster by not having to mail your documents and waiting for them to be received by the Social Security Administration.

It is advised that you document when you submit your application and have hard copies of the documents on file. This will help the process run smoothly if, by chance, your documents were not electronically received.

BRENDA'S STORY

Brenda was 55 years old when her Crohn's disease flared up and she found it impossible to continue working in her job as a phlebotomist. Since she had worked since she was 20 years old, Brenda was confident that she had accumulated sufficient work credits to receive Social Security Disability. Brenda applied on her own and was shocked when she was denied benefits due to insufficient work credits. Brenda contacted an attorney to delve into the details of the denial before she appealed her case. After a thorough interview with the attorney, she discovered that Brenda had not reported income under her maiden name since she had married 5 years ago. Without informing the Social Security office of her name change and filing her taxes with her husband, there had been no documented record of those years worked. Brenda's attorney assisted her with proving her name change and correcting her work history with the Social Security Administration. As a direct result of legal intervention, Brenda's benefits were approved.

The Waiting Period

The most difficult part of applying for Social Security Disability benefits is waiting for the outcome of your case. It is already challenging to live with a severe disability. Not having enough money to pay your necessary expenses can increase your stress level and aggravate your disability. This may add to your disability and limit your ability to complete daily tasks.

Only a few Social Security Disability applicants have the opportunity to receive an income from a long-term disability insurance policy or a worker's compensation claim. A majority of applicants have been living without a source of income for many months or years or their state disability benefits have sadly run out. This forces these Social Security Disability applicants to live off of the savings that they have accumulated over their lifetime. It can also be very difficult to pay your necessary expenses if your family is now living on only one income. This can have a drastic effect on your finances and your ability to pay your bills. Some applicants that have lived for many years without an income unfortunately had their vehicles repossessed, lost their homes in foreclosure, and were forced to live with family members or on the streets. You are at the mercy of the Social Security Administration when you are waiting to receive benefits. It may be a difficult process, but you must maintain hope that you will eventually receive your Social Security Disability benefits.

Applying for Social Security Disability benefits can take many months or even years. It is frustrating when you must wait for the Social Security Administration to make a decision on the outcome of your case. During that time, your expenses may start to pile up and become very overwhelming. A way to help you reduce the stress of worrying about the many bills that need to be paid is to negotiate with your creditors. When you do not pay your bills on time, they will be sent to a collection agency. Collection agencies can become very persistent in trying to obtain money for the delinquent expenses. Some of the larger collection agencies may allow you to suspend payments for a certain period of time if you explain your situation. If the collection agency knows you are suffering from a severe disability and are applying for Social Security Disability benefits, they may allow you to pay your bills at a later date.

Many people who apply for Social Security Disability benefits may have a mortgage or car loan. If you are struggling to make the payments on your house or vehicle, you may be able to suspend your payments. Contact your home or vehicle lender, before your loan becomes delinquent, to ask if they offer a forbearance program. Most programs will typically last three to six months to give you an opportunity to catch up with late payments. This will help you alleviate the stress of losing your vehicle or home and allow you some time to determine if you have been approved to receive disability benefits.

If you are unable to work and have applied for Social Security Disability benefits, you may be eligible to take part in your state's welfare program. This program helps people who are struggling to pay their expenses. Some of the benefits you may receive from a welfare program are food stamps and income to support your dependent children. When you do successfully win your Social Security Disability case, you may have to reimburse the state welfare agency for any money you received.

Some Social Security Disability applicants may not have an opportunity to suspend their mortgage payments and may unfortunately lose their house to foreclosure. This can be a devastating time filled with emotion and stress. You may consider moving in with close friends or family who may help you through this upsetting event. Your county or town may also offer shelter to people who have lost their home. They will be able to give you a place to stay without having to live on the streets. Shelters try to accommodate as many people as they can, but some require you to provide proof that you are looking for work. This would be difficult for you, since you have a severe disability that has forced you to apply for Social Security Disability benefits.

Many Social Security Disability applicants are struggling to pay their expenses. They want to make sure their family is housed and well fed. This can be difficult when you are disabled and unable to work. Some Social Security Disability applicants decide they should try to find a job they are able to accomplish, even if they can only do the job for a few weeks. Going back to work while you are applying for Social Security Disability benefits can be a dangerous decision. When your case is reviewed by the Administrative Law Judge he will see that you went back to work. In most instances, this would allow your case to be denied; to the court, since you are able to work, you do not need disability benefits. The amount of time you work at this job will not be considered, even if it was only for one day.

CHRISTINA'S STORY

Christina worked as a commercial real estate agent for the past ten years. She suddenly began experiencing vertigo. This can be a severe disability, because it can cause you to feel constantly dizzy and makes it very difficult to maintain your balance as you walk. This debilitating condition forced Christina to stop working as a real estate agent, which involves continuous walking and movement.

Christina decided she needed to apply for Social Security Disability benefits to help her through this tough time in her life. While she was waiting for her disability benefits to be approved, her expenses and bills continued to pile up. Christina decided she needed to make a small salary to help pay for the bills. Her friend offered her a job as a real estate agent at his new housing development. The job only required Christina to sit in one of the model homes and greet prospective buyers who came to look at the homes. She only worked on the weekends and received a small salary.

Christina was eventually sent a notice saying that she could meet with the Administrative Law Judge to review her case. She decided that she did not need an attorney to represent her when she met with judge, because she thought she would be approved for disability benefits. When the judge began the hearing, he continued to ask Christina why she went back to work when she was applying for Social Security Disability benefits. He could not figure how she could work every weekend and still be considered disabled. Since Christina decided not to have an attorney represent her, she did not know how to answer the judge's questions. In the end Christina was denied disability benefits.

Attending school can also negatively affect your ability to receive disability benefits. Even if you think attending school will help you in your future, it may affect your ability to win your case for disability benefits. The case reviewers and the Administrative Law Judge may think if you are able to attend school on a regular basis you do not need to receive disability benefits. They will say you would be able to hold a job that would pay for your expenses.

ROBERT'S STORY

Robert was a school teacher for twenty years and enjoyed going to work every day. He always wanted to make a difference by helping children succeed in school. One afternoon when Robert was walking his dog after it snowed, he slipped on a patch of ice causing him to lose his balance and fall. As a result of his fall, Robert broke is back. He needed to have surgery and go through several years of physical therapy to live a normal life. During this time, Robert had to quit the job he loved and move in with his children. They helped pay his expenses as he tried to regain his ability to return to work.

After several years of physical therapy, Roberts' condition was not getting any better and he decided he would not be able to return to work as a teacher. His family suggested he apply for Social Security Disability benefits. After he was awarded Social Security Disability Income (SSDI), he was informed that he would be receiving retroactive benefits going back twelve months before he applied for disability benefits. Even though Robert was disabled for over three years he will only get a maximum of twelve months of retroactive disability benefits.

If Robert consulted with an attorney when he initially became injured, Robert may have begun receiving disability benefits earlier. He would not have missed out on over two years of disability benefits.

Receiving Your Benefits

It is a very joyful moment when you are notified that you will receive disability benefits. You will now have the security needed to live a calm life, without the worry of paying your necessary expenses. Having an income will help you to focus on your disability and living a joyful life. The Social Security Administration sets different timelines for receiving Social Security Disability Income

(SSDI) and Supplemental Security Income (SSI).

The amount of Social Security Disability Income (SSDI) you receive is based on how long you have worked and the amount of money you have invested into the Social Security Trust Fund. Each person who is awarded Social Security Disability Income (SSDI) will be given a different amount of benefits. The Social Security Administration uses a complex formula to determine your monthly disability benefit amount. Daggett Shuler will be able to help you identify the amount of Social Security Disability Income (SSDI) you may receive if you win your case.

If you have been approved for Supplemental Security Income (SSI) your benefits may begin the first full month after you filed your application for SSI. The receipt of SSI gives you the ability to start paying for your necessary expenses. You will not have to worry about how you will pay the bills and provide for your family.

Each year, the Social Security Administration sets the maximum amount of benefits you may receive for Supplemental Security Income (SSI). Since this Social Security program is considered a supplemental income, your current income will be used to determine the amount of benefits you may receive. Daggett Shuler, Attorneys at Law will be able to help you determine how much income you may receive if you are awarded Supplemental Security Income (SSI).

You may also qualify to receive health coverage while you receive Social Security Disability benefits. Having a medical health plan will help to cover the costs of your future medical needs and care. Receiving health insurance will give you the security of knowing that if you do need medical treatment or care, you will not have to use your entire life savings. The type of coverage and the process is different for people receiving SSDI benefits and SSI. If you are receiving SSDI benefits, you may be eligible to receive Medicare coverage. This will help you to pay for your hospital and doctor bills. The downside to receiving Medicare coverage is you must wait twenty-four (24) months until you are allowed to apply for Medicare health coverage. If you are suffering from chronic kidney disease requiring regular dialysis, Amyotrophic Lateral Sclerosis (ALS), or are waiting for a transplant you may be covered by Medicare immediately. SSI recipients are eligible to receive Medicaid health coverage without a waiting period. This may be helpful for SSI members who need to see their doctor or hospital frequently.

CHAPTER SIX

APPEALING YOUR CASE

The application process to receive Social Security Disability benefits consists of five levels. You begin the process by submitting the required forms and documents to the Social Security Administration. If you are denied disability benefits after you file the application, you may appeal your case four times in the following levels: Level Two: The Reconsideration Process, Level Three: Administrative Law Judge, Level Four: The Appeals Council, and lastly Level Five: The Federal Court. In this chapter we will discuss an overview of the appeal levels. This will give you an understanding of the appeals process and what you may need to go through in order to receive your Social Security Disability benefits.

Your Claim Has Been Denied

It can be very disappointing to open the letter from the Social Security Administration and discover that your application has been denied. You may feel as if all the hard work you have completed was for nothing. You should not allow yourself to believe that you have no hope in receiving your disability benefits. This is just one of many steps in the disability process and you will have more opportunities to pursue your disability benefits. Daggett Shuler, Attorneys at Law will be able to assist you in planning your case.

MARGARET'S STORY

While typing court records one day a 55-year-old transcriptionist had difficulty focusing on her documents. The news from her eye doctor was devastating when Margaret was told that her diagnosis of macular degeneration would eventually result in blindness. She was soon unable to continue working at the courthouse with her significantly impaired vision. Due to the fact that her position was sub-contracted, Margaret was ineligible to receive health insurance and unable to afford the medical treatment suggested by her physician.

Since the transcriptionist was familiar with government policies, she felt confident that she could apply for Social Security Disability benefits on her own. Unfortunately, Margaret received a denial letter from the Social Security Administration because they felt her vision was not impaired enough to qualify as a disability.

Margaret decided to hire an attorney to represent her during the appeal process. When Margaret's first appeal was denied she filed a Request for Hearing. Margaret's attorney designed a well documented case to be prepared for the court hearing. During the hearing, an expert medical witness testified that the claimant was unable to continue working in the highly technical job as a court transcriptionist due to her vision impairment. The argument was made to the Administrative Law Judge that her profession required perfect vision and that the possibility of her finding similar employment would be impossible. Her case was successfully appealed and the Administrative Law Judge ruled in her favor. She was awarded Social Security Disability benefits.

Level Two: The Reconsideration Process

It is disappointing to receive your letter stating that your claim has been denied. You should not become disappointed and feel as if you will never receive disability benefits. You will have other opportunities to appeal your case. When you receive your letter, you must carefully review it to learn why you were denied and what your next step should be in the application process. You should also keep in mind that you only have sixty (60) days from the date you receive your letter to appeal your case. If you allow the sixty (60) day period to run out, you will have to start the application process over from the beginning.

Often, your case has been denied because your medical providers did not submit the requested records, the medical records were not properly evaluated, your medical records were not up-to-date, or you did not provide the Social Security Administration with all the requested information. You are able to challenge the denial of your application during The Reconsideration Process. To increase your chances of winning your case, you should contact Daggett Shuler, Attorneys at Law at 1-800-815-5500 for a free consultation. We will help you through the process and design a plan of action personalized to your situation.

During The Reconsideration Process you will need to fill out and submit several forms stating that you are appealing your case. During this level, you need to describe your disability in detail and, if so, how your disability has worsened. The more detail you provide the Social Security Administration, the easier it will be for them to decide the outcome of your case. This is also an opportunity for you to include other medical documents that may not have been included in the initial application.

Level Three: Administrative Law Judge

You may appeal the denial of your claim for benefits at The Reconsideration Level by asking to have your case heard by an Administrative Law Judge. This level of the process is different than the previous levels because you must appear in court to state your case. Within sixty (60) days of the denial at the reconsideration level you must submit the required forms stating that you wish to appeal your case to an Administrative Law Judge. You will receive a hearing letter that will inform you of your case details including the hearing date and time. During this appeal level you must persuade a judge that you are disabled based on your medical records and testimony at the hearing. During this part of the process you should seek legal representation to help you in court.

ANGELA'S STORY

Angela was 54 years old when she needed to apply for disability benefits. Prior to applying for disability benefits, Angela had two knee replacement surgeries. Even after the surgeries she was still having difficulty standing and walking. When she filled out her employment history, Angela told the Social Security Administration that she was a car saleswoman for fifteen years. She also stated that prior to selling cars she worked as a toll-booth collector for four years.

Angela was not approved for disability benefits, because the Social Security Administration said she could still work as a toll-booth collector. This job did not involve walking and would not affect her knees. The Social Security Administration should not have used her job as a toll-booth collector to determine if she was qualified to receive disability benefits because that job was performed over fifteen years before she applied. Angela discussed her situation with an attorney who agreed to represent her during the court hearing. The attorney was able to explain to the Administrative Law Judge that Angela's case should not have included her job as a toll-booth collector because it occurred more than fifteen years ago. When Angela appealed her claim with an attorney representing her in front of the Administrative Law Judge, she was awarded her disability benefits.

During the Administrative Law Judge level of the appeal process, you will have the opportunity to present your testimony by describing how your disability has affected your ability to hold a job. During the hearing, you will also have the opportunity to have a witness testify about your disability. The witness can give their firsthand account of your daily struggles and why you deserve to receive Social Security Disability benefits. Daggett Shuler, Attorneys at Law will be able to prepare you for your court appearance and walk you through the process of appearing in court. We will also be able to assist in finding a witness who can describe how your disability has affected your life. Having an attorney present with you in the court room will reassure you that you are not going through the appeal process alone. We will be there to make sure you have the best chance of receiving your disability benefits.

Level Four: The Appeals Council

If you did not successfully obtain your Social Security Disability benefits from the Administrative Law Judge, you still have another opportunity. You may continue through the process and appeal your case to the Appeals Council. After you are informed that the Administrative Law Judge has denied your claim to receive disability benefits, you only have sixty (60) days to appeal your case. This is a very important part of the appeal process because if you let the sixty (60) day time period expire you must file a new application. To appeal the judge's unfavorable decision you will need to submit the required forms stating that you wish to appeal your case to the Appeals Council.

The appeals court level of the application process is slightly different than the Administrative Law Judge level. At this level, the judge reviewing your case may never personally meet with you and discuss your disability. Their job in the process is to review the documentation describing your disability from the Administrative Law Judge. Sometimes the Appeals Court Judge will request further factual information describing your disability and how it affects your ability to work at a substantial job. The judge may consult physicians, often called medical support staff, or vocational experts. The consultants will state their opinion of the severity of your disability. The Appeals Council Judge will include the new information in your case as documented information.

This level of the appeals process may last several months until a decision is made by the Appeals Council Judge. If your case is approved, you will be granted Social Security Disability benefits. This will relieve you of the stress and worries of trying to pay your necessary expenses. There is still a chance that your claim does not get approved and you are denied disability benefits. The Appeals Council Judge will determine that your case does not need to be altered and the Administrative Law Judge's decision will stand as the final decision.

Level Five: Federal District Court

The final level in the appeal process is Federal District Court. You can proceed to this level if you are denied Social Security Disability benefits and the Appeals Council denies your request for review. At the Federal District Court level, you file a lawsuit against the Social Security Administration. This level can be very time consuming and involves advanced knowledge of the United States legal system. You will need an attorney to represent you during your Federal District Court appeal. Daggett Shuler, Attorneys at Law will be there to represent you and help you win your case. You may contact us at 1-800-815-5500 for a free consultation of your case.

To continue the appeal process to the Federal District Court level, you must file a lawsuit in your district court within sixty (60) days of when the Appeals Council denies your request for review. This is an important part of the appeal process because if you let the sixty (60) day period go by you will need to start your claim over by filing a new application. The judge in the Federal District Court will review your case to determine if any legal errors occurred and if the unfavorable decision was supported by substantial evidence. Many claimants do not get to this level of the appeal process since it takes a large amount of time and energy. It also takes many months or years to travel through the levels of appeal. You should discuss your situation with Daggett Shuler, Attorneys at Law to decide the steps you should take in the appeal process.

CHAPTER SEVEN

THE HEARING

Applying for Social Security Disability benefits can be a challenging and frustrating process. It involves compiling a well documented case and being prepared to answer any questions that arise. After you apply for disability benefits your case may be denied at the initial level. In Chapter Six: Appealing your Case, you were able to review the ways you can appeal your claim if it is denied after you file the application. If this happens, then you can file a request for reconsideration. If the reconsideration is denied, you can appeal the decision to an Administrative Law Judge. At this level your case will be reviewed by a judge who may use medical and vocation advisors to determine your case. This review is conducted during a hearing when you appear in a court room in front of the judge. This chapter will give you a preview of what you can expect at the hearing. Knowing all the details of the hearing will eliminate all of the surprises and prepare you for what will occur.

Walking Through the Hearing

At the hearing level you will have an opportunity to meet with a judge in court to discuss your disability and how it has affected your ability to work. This is a chance for you to explain why you deserve disability benefits and how these benefits will help you live a normal life. You may think it is a daunting task to meet with an Administrative Law Judge in court, but it may be the moment when you are approved to receive disability benefits. We will give you an overview of the court hearing and what you may face. This will give you a better understanding of the court system and the advantages of having an attorney with you during the hearing.

Most Social Security Disability claimants who reach the

hearing level believe they will be meeting the judge in a large court room surrounded by many people. This is usually not the normal setup for a Social Security Disability hearing. The majority of Social Security Administration court rooms are housed in office buildings where they have created an informal court room. During the hearing, there will only be a few people present. There will not be a jury, an opposing party or even an audience of people in the court room. Usually the court room will include the Administrative Law Judge, the judge's assistant, a medical and/ or vocational expert, personal witnesses, your attorney, and yourself. There is no need to feel overwhelmed with the thought of going to a court room and meeting the judge. It is an informal situation where you have an opportunity to describe your disability and how it has affected your ability to work.

The Administrative Law Judge (ALJ) that you meet during a hearing will be appointed by the Social Security Administration. They have been assigned to handle Social Security Disability cases that have been appealed to the hearing level of the appeal process. The Administrative Law Judge is not part of any previous Social Security Administration office that denied your disability benefits. It is their job to review all of the evidence and not rely on any previous decisions about your claim. Before the Administrative Law Judges worked for the Social Security Administration, they may have been in private practice and represented Social Security Disability claimants who were trying to receive disability benefits. Other Administrative Law Judges may have been an Administrative Law Judge in a different department of our government, such as military cases within the United States Army.

During the hearing, your attorney will be with you to ensure you know exactly what you should do and say. It can be difficult at times to answer the questions the Administrative Law Judge asks you. Having Daggett Shuler represent you in court will give you the resources and knowledge needed to have a successful court hearing. The Administrative Law Judge may decide to include a medical expert, a vocational expert, or both during the hearing. This will give the judge added information needed to make an accurate decision on your disability claim. The judge will usually ask the medical or vocational expert to give their opinion about your disability and how it has affected your ability to work. They will also be asked several other questions regarding the types of jobs you may be qualified for or the details of your previous jobs.

Your attorney will determine if all the information that the medical or vocational experts discuss is accurate and relevant to your disability. It can be overwhelming to determine if everything the judge and experts are saying is correct and they are abiding by the applicable regulations. Having an attorney who has studied the legal system and Social Security Disability law for many years will relieve you of this stress. You will be able to concentrate on staying calm through the hearing and clearly answering all the questions the judge asks you.

When the Administrative Law Judge is finished questioning the medical or vocational experts you will be asked questions about your disability and how it has affected your ability to work. The judge may ask you questions about your work experience over the last fifteen years and why you needed to leave those jobs. This will give the judge an overview of your work history and if you have the ability to return to any of your previous jobs. You may also be asked questions about your medical history and when your disability began. The judge wants to make sure all the information about your disability is presented and that what you say during the hearing is the same as the information you submitted when you applied for Social Security Disability benefits. You may be asked to describe, in detail, your disability, the affects it has on you, and any treatments you have received to alleviate your disability. You always need to explain your story and your disability using the same details. This will show that you are actually suffering from a severe disability and are telling the truth. Your attorney will prepare you for the hearing by reviewing some questions that you may be asked.

During the hearing, you will be scrutinized by the Administrative Law Judge the entire time you are in the court room. This may seem frightening or even stressful, but the judge will use everything they see as information to determine whether you are disabled. When the hearing begins and the judge starts asking you questions about your disability and how it has affected your ability to work, you should clearly and calmly answer the questions. Many Social Security Disability claimants become argumentative or shocked at the types of questions the judge is asking. You are only being asked questions about the details of your disability so the judge can understand your medical condition and how it affects your daily activities. You should never become argumentative or uncooperative during the hearing. This could lead to a rescheduling of the hearing or the denial of your claim for disability benefits. If any part of the questioning does not seem relevant or accurate about your disability, your attorney will make sure you are given the opportunity to explain yourself. Having Daggett Shuler, Attorneys at Law represent you during your hearing will make the process less stressful and ensure that all of the relevant information in your case is discussed.

MICHAEL'S STORY

Michael decided he would attend the disability hearing on his own without the help of an attorney. While the judge was questioning Michael, he responded disrespectfully and angrily. The judge made the decision to stop the hearing. He strongly suggested that Michael hire an attorney to represent him and rescheduled the hearing.

When Michael retold this story to an attorney, Michael explained he had been upset with the judge's questions. The attorney agreed to take the case on the condition that Michael would follow his advice and behave properly at the hearing.

During the hearing, Michael remained calm, spoke respectfully, and made an excellent impression on the judge during the questioning. With the help of an attorney Michael was able to win the case and receive disability benefits.

Having an experienced attorney represent you at your hearing will give you the best chance of winning your case. Your attorney will review the hearing process with you and give you advice on how you should act during the hearing. Body language can be very important as well as how you answer the questions you will be asked. The Administrative Law Judge's job is to investigate the facts to determine whether you are truly disabled. Your conduct must be a positive part of your case.

ALLEGRA'S STORY

A 46 year old woman, Allegra, went to a law firm to ask an attorney to represent her during a disability hearing. Allegra had worked as an executive secretary for over fifteen years. Her job had included writing short-hand dictations, data entry, and an extensive amount of typing. Two years ago, Allegra was severely injured in a skiing accident. She suffered neck and back injuries which caused arm and finger numbness. Allegra found it almost impossible to do the fine motor skills necessary to continue working as an executive secretary. All of the testing and reports from her physicians supported her claims of arm and hand numbness.

Allegra's female attorney noticed the lovely, intricately woven braids of her hair. Her attorney casually asked Allegra where she had her hair done. She replied that she did her own hair and that she was very proud of it. What seemed like a superficial conversation between two women was actually an important observation on the attorney's part as a lawyer. If this same question had been asked by the judge during the disability hearing, Allegra would have lost her case.

Upon further questioning, Allegra admitted that it took her hours to braid her hair. When the finger numbness started, she would take a break and try again later. Although Allegra was proud of her hair, it had taken her all day to accomplish this one hour procedure. This was an important fact to discuss with the judge at her hearing.

Judges are very observant of body language and the smallest of details. The Administrative Law Judge may ask a claimant if they were able to knit, sew, tie their shoes, or comb their hair. If the judge thought Allegra was capable of fine motor skill intricacies, the judge would feel she could continue to perform the skills necessary as an executive secretary and deny her claim.

Having an attorney represent you during your court hearing will give you the needed resources to win your case. You will be advised about all the details involved in winning your case based on observed body language.

Medical and Vocational Experts

During the hearing the Administrative Law Judge may want the assistance of a medical or vocational expert. If so, the judge will want to have all of the medical and other evidence for the experts to review. Your attorney will make sure that all of the evidence is available for the experts to review because the judge may ask the medical or vocational experts for their opinions on certain issues important to your case. For example, the medical expert may explain medical records to the judge and explain how your medical condition affects your ability to work. This gives the Administrative Law Judge a better understanding of the disability and how it affects you. Often the medical expert will be asked to give their opinion of the severity of your medical condition. They may be asked to compare the evidence and information about your disability to the Listing of Impairments. An overview of the Listing of Impairments can be reviewed in Chapter Two: Understanding Common Disabilities or on the Social Security Administration's website at SSA.gov. If the medical expert believes your disability meets the Listing of Impairments, the hearing may end and you could be awarded disability benefits. Sometimes, the medical expert does not believe your disability meets the Listing of Impairments. If that is the case, the Administrative Law Judge may ask the medical expert to determine the severity of your disability and your work limitations. The judge wants to hear all the evidence and determine if it supports your disability claim.

The Administrative Law Judge may also ask a vocational expert to be present during the hearing. The vocational expert may be used if the medical expert believes your disability does not meet the Listing of Impairments. The Administrative Law Judge will want to know what your limitations are if you do not meet the requirements of the Listings of Impairments. The vocational expert will explain to the Administrative Law Judge the type of work you did in the past and if you have the ability to return to one of your previous jobs. If the vocational expert believes you are unable to return to one of your previous jobs, then consideration will be given to whether you can return to work at any other type of job. The vocational expert will explain whether you have acquired any new skills or abilities that would help you return to work. The Administrative Law Judge will ask the vocational expert questions pertaining to your ability to work during the hearing. Your attorney will also be given the opportunity to question the vocational expert and can make sure the judge has all of the relevant information needed to make a decision in your case.

The Power of an Attorney

Many Social Security Disability claimants believe they can file an application and successfully appeal a denial. They often feel their disability is clear and easy to identify so their application will be approved. This may seem as if it is the perfect scenario, but most applicants face a difficult battle towards their disability benefits. Having an attorney represent you through the application process can help relieve the stress you are under and let you focus on your health and family. You may face difficult questions during the application process and your attorney will be able to answer these questions and guide you through the appeal process to ensure you are prepared for any challenge you may face. They will make sure all your documentation is accurate to give you the best chance of success. Having Daggett Shuler, Attorneys at Law represent you will make the application process simple and free of stress that may aggravate your disability. We have extensive knowledge of the laws associated with Social Security Disability and know the correct legal action to take throughout the application process. Our goal is to ensure you receive the Social Security Disability benefits you deserve.

If the Administrative Law Judge asks a medical expert to be present during the hearing, your attorney will have the opportunity to ask questions. This will be a time to ensure all the medical evidence is considered in your case to determine if you are disabled. If the medical expert does not believe your medical condition meets one of the Listing of Impairments, your attorney will question the medical expert about your medical condition to make sure the Administrative Law Judge has all of the information about your case. You will not have to worry about knowing if the medical expert made their decision using all the available evidence. Your attorney will be present at the hearing to help you win your case by questioning the medical expert.

During some hearings, the Administrative Law Judge will ask a vocational expert to be present. The vocational expert will be used to determine your abilities and if you have the ability to work at specific jobs. During the hearing, the judge will ask the vocational expert to list jobs that you may be able to perform with your physical and mental limitations. Sometimes, the vocational expert will list jobs that do not take into account all of your limitations. Your attorney will be present to question the vocational expert and to make sure all of your limitations are considered. Having an attorney represent you at the hearing will take the pressure off of you and ensure that all of the information is considered by the judge.

CHAPTER EIGHT

SOCIAL SECURITY DISABILITY MYTHS

If you are applying for Social Security Disability benefits you may have heard some myths about the process. For example, one myth is that Social Security claimants are not allowed to work when they apply for disability benefits or that Social Security Disability cases are processed in three to four months. In this chapter we will review these myths and other common Social Security Disability myths. This will give you a better understanding of the Social Security Disability process and what you can expect.

Everyone is Denied the First Time They Apply

It may seem that everyone who applies for Social Security Disability benefits is denied the first time they apply. This is actually not true. The Social Security Administration will not automatically deny your application. They do, however, deny a majority of claimants the first time they apply. This is because most claimants do not submit all the required forms and documents related to their disability claim. By having Daggett Shuler, Attorneys at Law working for you it will increase your chances of winning your case when the application is filed because we will make sure the correct forms are submitted and all the necessary information is provided to the Social Security Administration.

Specific Diseases Automatically Qualify a Person for Disability Benefits

Sadly this myth is not true. Everyone who applies for Social Security Disability benefits must go through the same process to receive their benefits. If this myth was true, it would make receiving disability benefits an easier process without the stress of worrying if your claim will be approved. The Social Security Administration only uses your medical information, provided by your healthcare provider, to make the decision. The information provided must be accurate and thorough to give you the best chance of receiving disability benefits.

Younger Adults Cannot Qualify for Disability Benefits

Younger individuals, in their twenties and thirties, often believe they cannot qualify for Social Security Disability benefits. If you have worked enough to be insured and you have a disability that will last at least twelve months or result in death, then you can apply for Social Security Disability benefits.

Social Security Disability Cases are Processed in Three to Four Months

After the application is filed it usually takes 2-3 months to get the initial determination. If the initial determination is a denial and the reconsideration is denied as well and a hearing has to be requested, then it can take a year or more to get a hearing date before an Administrative Law Judge. However, each case is different so the amount of time each case takes to be concluded is different as well.

I am Clearly Disabled, So I Do Not Need an Attorney to Win My Case

Many claimants believe their disability is obvious so they feel like an attorney is unnecessary to win their case. This is an incorrect assumption. The Social Security Administration and the Administrative Law Judge that reviews your case may not see your situation the same way as you do. They will look at your case from a legal perspective instead of your personal experience and perspective. Working with an attorney will help you build a case by explaining it to the Social Security Administration and judges how your disability has affected you from a legal perspective. Your attorney will put the facts of your case in the proper legal context. This will give you the best chance of winning your case.

I Know Someone Who is on Social Security Disability, But Does Not Appear Disabled

Social Security Disability claimants are all over the country and each case is unique. Someone who is receiving disability benefits may appear quite healthy, but they are actually suffering from significant medical impairments that are not clearly visible. For example, they may suffer from a disabling mental illness while being physically healthy and able to do many physical activities.

My Friend Received Social Security Disability Benefits and We Have the Same Illness, So I Should Also Receive Social Security Disability Benefits

Even if you know someone who suffers from the same medical problems as you and receives disability benefits does not mean the Social Security Administration will automatically approve your claim. Each application is unique and is never compared to other applications. Your disability will be analyzed and compared to the medical and other evidence that is submitted in support of your claim.

My Social Security Disability Claim Was Denied, So I Must Not Be Disabled

If your initial application for Social Security Disability benefits is not approved, you should not give up. You may still have a good disability claim. Remember, the majority of disability applications are denied. When you applied for Social Security Disability benefits you may not have included enough information to prove your claim. An attorney will be able to help you through the application process and get you the disability benefits you deserve. They will compile a well documented case that includes all the required forms and evidence to support your disability claim.

CHAPTER NINE

FREQUENTLY ASKED QUESTIONS

This chapter will highlight the twenty most frequently asked questions about Social Security Disability benefits. It will cover many topics, such as the types of Social Security Disability programs, applying for disability benefits, and appealing your claim.

What is the definition of disability used by the Social Security Administration?

Disability is defined by the Social Security Act as the "inability to engage in any substantial gainful activity by reason of any medically determinable physical or mental impairment, which can be expected to result in death or has lasted or can be expected to last for a continuous period of not less than twelve months."

How many types of Social Security Disability benefit programs does the Social Security Administration offer?

The Social Security Administration offers five different types of disability benefits:

- Social Security Disability Insurance (SSDI) is the most common type of disability benefit offered by the Social Security Administration. Anyone who has worked at least five of the last ten years and is disabled may apply for SSDI benefits.

- Supplemental Security Income (SSI) is a benefit program designed for disabled individuals who have a limited amount of income and resources. The Social Security

Administration does not require SSI applicants to have worked in the past.

- Disabled Widow's and Widower's Benefits are provided for individuals who are age 50 or older and have become disabled shortly after the death of their spouse. These disability benefits can be received only if their late spouse worked long enough to be insured by the Social Security Administration.

- Disabled Adult Child Benefits are provided for disabled children whose parents are either receiving Social Security Disability or Social Security retirement benefits or who are deceased. To be eligible for disability benefits, the child must have become disabled before age 22. The Social Security Administration does not take into account the recipient's income and resources.

- Supplemental Security Income (SSI) can also be awarded to disabled children under the age of 18. The definition of disabled for children is different from that of adults. Daggett Shuler, Attorneys at Law will help you determine if you may be eligible to receive SSI as a child.

How do I apply for Social Security Disability benefits?

The Social Security Administration provides three ways for you to apply for Social Security Disability benefits. The easiest and most direct way to apply is to go to your nearest Social Security Administration office. This will give you an opportunity to file a claim in person and know that they received your claim. You may also contact the Social Security Administration by calling their toll-free number at 1-800-772-1213. The third option is to file a claim for disability benefits on the Social Security Administration's website at www.ssa.gov.

When I become disabled how long do I have to wait before I can file for Social Security Disability Benefits?

You can file an application for Social Security Disability benefits as soon as you become disabled. Many claimants make the mistake of waiting months or even years after they became disabled to apply. This only delays your receipt of disability benefits. The sooner you apply, the faster you receive your disability benefits. You should not apply for disability benefits if you experience a minor injury that will not affect you for at least twelve months. If you believe your injury will keep you from working for at least twelve months you should not hesitate to apply for disability benefits.

Can I receive Social Security Disability Benefits and workers' compensation at the same time?

You can receive both workers' compensation and Social Security Disability benefits at the same time. The Social Security Disability benefits will be offset based on the amount of benefits you receive from workers' compensation. This means that your Social Security Disability benefits will be reduced depending on the amount of benefits you receive from workers' compensation. In certain states, your workers' compensation benefits will be reduced based on the amount of Social Security Disability benefits you receive.

Is there a way to see if the Social Security Administration will consider me disabled?

Applying for Social Security Disability benefits is a difficult decision that you ultimately must make on your own. There is no way to know if you will be approved for disability benefits before applying. The Social Security Administration will analyze your disability to see if you qualify for disability benefits. Social Security Disability attorneys may make a prediction on the outcome of your case, but they will never be truly sure if you will win your case. Having an attorney review your case will increase your chances of being approved for disability benefits.

I have several health problems, but each problem alone does not make me disabled. When I combine all my health problems together I am disabled. Can I get Social Security Disability benefits?

The Social Security Administration will review your case and analyze all your health problems. They will determine how they affect your ability to work individually and as a whole. If the Social Security Administration believes all of your health problems together affect your ability to work you may be approved for disability benefits.

How does the Social Security Administration determine if I am disabled?

The Social Security Administration uses the sequential evaluation discussed earlier to determine if you are disabled. They review the medical and other evidence in your case and take into consideration your vocational factors, i.e., your age, education, and work experience. This information is used to determine whether you can do any of your past jobs or any other work in the national economy.

Who decides if I am disabled?

When you submit your application for Social Security Disability benefits, your claim will be sent to a case examiner in your state's Disability Determination Services office. The case examiner will review your claim and consult medical and vocational professionals to determine if you are disabled. If your claim gets denied, you can appeal your case by requesting reconsideration. At the reconsideration level a different case examiner will review your claim to determine if they believe you are disabled. If your claim is denied at the reconsideration level, you can appeal your case by requesting a hearing. At this level an Administrative Law Judge will review your case without being bound by the prior unfavorable determinations. At the hearing you will be given the opportunity to speak to the judge and explain why you are disabled. Having an attorney present will help you explain your disability and give you a better chance of winning your case.

How can I improve my chances of winning my Social Security Disability case?

The most important thing to remember is to fill out your application completely when you start the process. You also need to make sure you complete all of the required documents and forms that the Social Security Administration needs to process your claim. This will help to speed up the application process. Many claimants do not adequately describe their disability when they apply. This makes it difficult for the Social Security Administration to reach a decision in your case. You need to make sure you include a description of your physical and any psychological problems that interfere with your ability to work. You should not be embarrassed about describing your disability and how it has affected your ability to work.

How much will I receive from the Social Security Administration if I am approved for Social Security Disability benefits?

Each Social Security Disability program determines the amount of benefits you can receive using different formulas. Social Security Disability Insurance (SSDI) benefits are based on the amount of time you have worked in the past and the income you earned. Disabled Widow's and Widower's Benefits are based on the amount of time the deceased spouse worked and their earnings. Disabled Adult Child Benefits are based on the amount of time the child's parents worked and how much they earned. Supplemental Security Income (SSI) is calculated differently from the other disability programs. The Social Security Administration sets a base amount each year for SSI. If you are receiving other income, the SSI may be reduced.

Why does the Social Security Administration deny so many claims for disability benefits?

As discussed above, the process for applying for Social Security Disability benefits is complex and complicated. Many people who apply for Social Security Disability benefits fail to complete the necessary forms and they fail to provide the Social Security Administration with all of the information it needs to make a decision. Additionally, as claims move their way through the different appeal levels the Social Security Administration has medical and vocational professionals that it can use to evaluate claims from its perspective. Having an attorney help you will ensure that the proper forms are submitted and that all of the information that supports your claim is provided to the Social Security Administration. This will give you the best chance of having your disability claim approved.

How long does it take to get a hearing on a Social Security Disability claim?

Each case is different so it is impossible to know exactly how long it will take to get a hearing scheduled in your claim. The amount of time it takes can vary depending on the region of country in which you live and the hearing office that has jurisdiction over your claim. Generally, it takes about a year from the date you request a hearing for it to be scheduled. However, your attorney should be able to give you a good estimate of how long it will take based on the facts in your case and the hearing office that will handle your claim.

How is the Social Security Disability hearing in front of an Administrative Law Judge conducted?

Social Security Disability hearings are informal proceedings that involve a few people. There is usually a judge, the judge's assistant who may control a tape recorder, yourself, and your attorney. During some cases the Administrative Law Judge will have a vocational or medical expert present to testify about specific parts of your case. Your case will not involve a jury and there will not be any spectators present in the hearing. The Social Security Administration will not be represented by an attorney. The proceeding is more of a fact finding inquiry focused on your disability and why you believe you should receive Social Security Disability benefits.

What are my chances of winning if I attend a hearing before an Administrative Law Judge?

It may seem like many claimants get denied the first time they apply for disability benefits. At the initial application level about seventy-five percent of all Social Security Disability applications are denied. If you appeal your case to the hearing level where an Administrative Law Judge will make the decision, you have about a fifty percent chance of winning your case. Your chances of winning at the hearing level are better because you have an attorney helping you and because you have the opportunity to present your case to the Administrative Law Judge. Before this level in the process, the Social Security Administration only considered your documentation and you did not have the right to present your case to the decision maker. This makes it all the more important to have good representation at the hearing.

Can I appeal my case if the Administrative Law Judge denies my claim for disability benefits?

If you receive an unfavorable decision from the Administrative Law Judge, you have the right to appeal your case to the Appeals Council. You should consider having an attorney represent you if you decide to appeal your case to the Appeals Court. Daggett Shuler, Attorneys at Law can assist you in the appeal process. Contact us at 1-800-815-5500 to begin your free consultation.

What is the Appeals Council?

If the Administrative Law Judge issues an unfavorable decision, then you have the right to appeal your case to the Appeals Council. The Appeals Council will review your appeal to determine whether it will review the judge's decision. The Appeals Council is located in Falls Church, Virginia. You and your attorney will not have to travel to the Appeals Council. They will review the documentation that is already part of your case and any additional documentation that you submit with your appeal.

Can I appeal my case beyond the Social Security Administration to federal court?

You can appeal your Social Security Disability case to federal court. If the Appeals Council upholds the Administrative Law Judge's decision, you can file a civil lawsuit in United States District Court. If the district court upholds the Administrative Law Judge's decision you have the right to appeal your case to the court of appeals. If the court of appeals upholds the judge's decision you can ask the United States Supreme Court to review your case. Each year the Supreme Court hears about one Social Security Disability case and turns down the requests from all the rest.

If I receive Social Security Disability benefits and I am eventually able to return to work, am I allowed to return to work?

Absolutely. You can and most claimants do return to work. The Social Security Administration encourages individuals who are receiving disability benefits to return to work. If you are receiving Social Security Disability Insurance (SSDI) Benefits, Disabled Widow's and Widower's Benefits, and Disabled Adult Child Benefits, you can receive your benefits after you return to work but this is an issue that you should discuss with your attorney to ensure that you do not create an overpayment.

I know someone who is receiving Social Security Disability benefits, but he does not look disabled. Why is the Social Security Administration giving him disability benefits?

Disabling impairments are often impossible to see. The Social Security Administration gives disability benefits to many people who look healthy. This is another reason why it is difficult for some people who are disabled to receive benefits. As an example, many people who are receiving disability benefits suffer from severe psychiatric illnesses. They can look physically healthy and are able to do simple tasks, such as mowing their lawn. In reality their psychiatric illness has kept them from working and supporting themselves and their families.

CONCLUSION

We wrote this book in order to give our current and potential clients a helpful and relatively detailed guide to the process of Social Security Disability benefits. We believe this book provides an overview of the disability process for people who have already decided to pursue a claim. It is also a helpful guide for those who want to know more about the Social Security Disability process before they choose to file a claim. As a potential client, you have the right to know what our firm will offer you and how we will guide you through the disability process. And if you become a client, you truly need to know these things about your case, for your own peace of mind and to help us make the case as successful as possible.

However, we know that no book can be detailed enough to address every client's situation. Each case, each disability, and each applicant is unique. That is why we want to once again encourage you to meet with us, if you have not already done so, because the better we know each other the more you will know what to expect when you become our client.

As Social Security Disability attorneys, we believe that helping people is the most important part of our work. A Social Security Disability case helps clients directly by providing them with the benefits they need to pay for life's expenses. There is nothing more fulfilling than being able to make a difference in someone's life. As our client, you are a partner in that work, and your participation is not just helpful — in many ways, it is essential. We hope that this book has helped you better understand what you can expect from your case, and your own role in making it a success.

Made in the USA
Monee, IL
04 November 2026

67387895R00046